# A Few Bruises Better

poems by

# Kevin Hinkle

Finishing Line Press
Georgetown, Kentucky

# A Few Bruises Better

Copyright © 2020 by Kevin Hinkle
ISBN 978-1-64662-209-2 First Edition
All rights reserved under International and Pan-American Copyright Conventions. No part of this book may be reproduced in any manner whatsoever without written permission from the publisher, except in the case of brief quotations embodied in critical articles and reviews.

## ACKNOWLEDGMENTS

*Survision* Issue 4 "I am a Rothko Painting," "Paintings in the Style of Francis Bacon by Francis Bacon," and "Wrong Turn"

Thank you to my workshop friends Michael McKeown Bondhus, Steven Cordova, and Walter Holland for their help in refining my work.

Publisher: Leah Maines
Editor: Christen Kincaid
Cover Art: Kevin Hinkle
Author Photo: Kevin Hinkle
Cover Design: Elizabeth Maines McCleavy

Printed in the USA on acid-free paper.
Order online: www.finishinglinepress.com
also available on amazon.com

Author inquiries and mail orders:
Finishing Line Press
P. O. Box 1626
Georgetown, Kentucky 40324
U. S. A.

# Table of Contents

Nocturnal Maneuvers ......................................................................... 1

Parts for Hire ..................................................................................... 2

Regression Therapy ........................................................................... 3

Pops .................................................................................................... 4

Motion to Remove ............................................................................. 5

Nightshade (or can I trust you Solanum?) ....................................... 6

Planting Hands .................................................................................. 7

I am a Rothko Painting ..................................................................... 8

Symptoms .......................................................................................... 9

Winter Grass ................................................................................... 10

Stuffed Owl ..................................................................................... 11

Paintings in the Style of Francis Bacon by Francis Bacon ............. 12

Reversal of Course .......................................................................... 13

Wrong Turn .................................................................................... 15

Suture .............................................................................................. 16

Drawn Blood .................................................................................. 17

Tug of War ...................................................................................... 18

Missing #2 ....................................................................................... 19

Perspectives on Goldfish ................................................................ 20

Some Things Have Seen Better Days ............................................ 21

*To Michael, my love, who inspires and supports me unwaveringly*

**Nocturnal Maneuvers**

Moonshine spills, and I worry about the stains.
The sofa's not as new as my lover
but I'll probably keep it longer.

Why can't I let the stains win?
What does it matter now the whites've yellowed,
and the blues've edged towards black?

The refrigerator's talking tonight—
haranguing me about my diet—what
I put in it; it only knows half the story.

Outside the grass is organizing.
My house is threatened by militias
marching towards the front door.

Opening, I hear the swishing
as the blades are parted. I can't see.
But I feel the movement. I crawl towards cover.

## Parts for Hire

Part of my foot went to Allesal. He liked it. Liked the way the veins pressed angrily against the skin as if they had other paths to follow, urgent duties to undertake. Their willingness to suffer had always impressed me.

I'll assume
they did the best they could.

But perhaps they weren't angry as I first surmised. Maybe their pronounced upward thrust was simply a service, a pressing up to provide a comfortable arch. Neither Allesal nor I was sure. Allesal wanted more; I demurred, insisted he pick and choose—

too much to one chopper, I argued,
would defeat the purpose.

Somehow the conversation veered philosophical. Allesal insisted that I didn't know where my feet were taking me. His desire, he argued, was a powerful testament to his commitment. That struck me as strange. Desire, commitment—co-conspirators?

## Regression Therapy

I've always had issues with my performance,
I told the doc. I have trouble until push
comes to shove.

> *Tell me more
> about your sexual experiences,
> he urged.*

When I was walking through a park on the way
home the other day—it hit me—how I humped a tree
when I was 12.

> *Relive that moment—my therapist was all ears.
> You're 12 again. Embrace it,*

so I ducked into a grove of trees, hugged the nearest one
and rubbed roughly. But I came away with nothing more than
bark.

> *I didn't mean it literally.
> I meant to go there in your memory
> and think about what you felt at the time.*

Now you tell me! Must I learn every lesson twice?

> *Apparently it wasn't obvious enough the first
> time—until it is, you're doomed to torn skin
> and public humiliation.*

Don't you mean I'm doomed to pain and humiliation either way?

*It doesn't help to be defeatist,* he responded.

## Pops

Today I'm "Pops"
to the smooth-faced barista—
impatient with my lagging
gait and the growing line.

*What can I get you, Pops?*

I consider moral outrage,
but I'm preoccupied—
stiff arms not swinging,
right leg not committed
to movement.

"Iced tea," I take my time replying.
*What size, Pops?*
"Bigger than you've got, Son,"
I think, but settle on "medium."

I want to leap
the counter to grapple respect
out of the pumped up
man-child, but

instead, I stand to the side
as he turns away, appreciating
his face unburdened
and the granite-veined hands
that roughly lift
my cup.

## Motion to Remove

It was The Corporation of Me annual meeting.
Allesal made a motion to remove me from the vote.
*Conflict of interest,* he argued. I was taking
too much ownership of my body. *It's on loan*
*he reminded me, but it's not yours in the way*
*you think it is.* I grumbled—at a loss
for logic.

It all boils down to control, I thought. It seems petty even—
kind of possession is 9/10ths of the law.
I seem to possess my body, and yet I have no control.
I can pump it full of stuff; I can pump it up, I can
cut it down, yet it can default on me at any time.

*I'm pretty sure you could use an upgrade,* Allesal
advised. "Is there any point in fighting planned obsolescence?"
I asked. *That's not up to you,* he answered as he handed me
the rules of incorporation.

## Nightshade (or can I trust you Solanum?)

Rumor says I need nightshade—that it's
the miracle cure. (Perhaps I exaggerate.)
I would investigate, but it
already surrounds me. I have nightshade
in spades—and it's embarrassing—like admitting
to gonorrhea.

I'm almost certain nightshade is mocking
me. Mostly, it resides in my imagination,
goading me into believing fairytales,
but occasionally it peeks over the collar of my cotton-
blend button-downs.

Even when it's not growing from my body,
flowering nightshade climbs the walls.
But is it there to keep me safe or prevent
me from escaping?

Every day, I take pains not to reveal
that my weakness is being weak.
I have neither prophet nor protector.

**Planting Hands**

Across the desert, landmines
were buried in unmarked soil
by planting hands long gone.

Move feet on automatic pilot.
Move feet and don't think
about a crash landing.

Once I watched chunks of a body
slingshot outward from its boney
core. Yellows, reds, and blues
unfurled like the colors of a
flag. But the jaunty colors faded
to charred sticks.

Move feet. Keep moving.
Hands can't be trusted.

**I am a Rothko Painting**

Canvas stretched across a frame, rough and dry.
I'm a Rothko painting—deep red,
brown, and orange. I'm February brooding,
suffocation from a lack of sun.

My therapist tells me to appreciate
my moods, to talk back and walk on. I nod...
but I'm Rothko painting.
I can't bear mirrors and self-contemplation.

I'm a Rothko painting, and it's difficult
to accept beauty's nuclear age.
I remind myself that sunlight varies by season,
meaning depends on context.

Rothko painted me layer on layer;
now let me hang and dry.

**Symptoms**

I want my feet
to be my feet—
to have a say
in where they go.

Quietly maybe, a soft step,
like an animal mama ready
to lift and carry you rough
but safe—a few bruises
better than a limb
caught in a trap.

I want my feet to know independence:
smooth dry stones, wet grass.
Let my feet build consensus
over my brain's objections.
Feet now bludgeon and earth
pushes up its sharpest replies.

## Winter Grass

Brittle grass, and I am haunted
by the thought of breaking bones.
But I hate winter's silent rebuke
as much as its bruising
and crackling.

Ten broken winters ago,
an ambulance pulled up
as if out on a lunch run,
past need for flashing lights,
too late for burning tires.

Now—winter again,
and I ask myself why
I remember. Like winter-
scarred grass, I recall
only the dying days.

**Stuffed Owl**

Much to observe when you're a stuffed
owl perched on dust and domestic turmoil.

Stuffed owl feathers begin to drift,
hypnotic rocking.

Momentary lull—stacks of books
and bills to balance.

Hoos cut like paper airplanes.

Claws dig into anything that settles;
pain finds ways to take root.

Feathers are light until they land. Just below,
damages are calculated in mop fibers.

Wide-eyed, unexpectedly, becomes
a meaningful descriptor.

**Paintings in the Style of Francis Bacon by Francis Bacon**

I've met myself coming round the bend and coming
round the bend, I've met myself. Direction
doesn't matter. I know when to expect it—never
in a mirror—always head on, not necessarily straight.
I still have not mastered self-expression.

Recently I noticed the floors hadn't been swept.
Furniture and boxes had halos announcing
their importance. Intimidated, I lost my train
of thought.

How can I improve on holiness when I've got a direct
line to existential hell? I get caught in texture and don't even
question colors. After a moment lost, I return
to my brushes and canvases.

I'm told a Francis Bacon is unmistakable. I'm told
that Francis Bacon is irreplaceable. If only there were
fortune cookies so that I could add "in bed." But I spend
too much time worrying.

My sex life has been a ripped canvas, repaired,
repainted. I'm not the only one who knows that Francis
Bacon is not so extraordinary. Only mangled images
from my imagination play out on canvas, but they aren't
'in bed.'

The days pass, and I paint my nightmares in thick layers.
I'm praised but don't know why.

**Reversal of Course**

At first the water planes the sidewalk smoothly
like a mid-winter sheet of ice. But then it begins
to rise up over itself as if trying to return to the hose—
a reverse ocean wave protesting gravity's top-down
pull. Why do individual drops of water come
together to form a wave?

I left something at home again—not my keys. I need
them to unlock the door from the inside, and I'm outside.
It's not my pills this time either. I know I've left
something at home again. I remembered and forgot.
How can I forget what I've just remembered?

The mouth of the hose spits and gurgles. Its neck
rears. Some of the water is fighting to get out while air
is fighting to get in—no clear consensus,
and the confrontation between the water and the air
claims the hose, now a charmed snake dancing;
the smooth stream no longer moves with ease.
Some water jumps; some falls to the ground.
Both end up tumbling head first into the gutter.

I'm in the house retracing my steps. The kitchen table
is a likely culprit. Bills, to-do lists, pill bottles gather like
friends kitchen-clustered at a party. Not a bill, not a pill.
In the living room stacks of books make sitting difficult.
Not a book. Not a folder.

I circle the bedroom reviewing visible surfaces; nothing
in my memory, nothing. I sit on the edge of the bed
to retrace my route and the earlier conversations
I had with myself. Clarity doesn't return. It's fallen
head long out of reach.

The water's completed its tumble now and has slammed leaves and bits of garbage into the gutter. There can be no return to starting. Clarity can't be claimed. Bits of leaves, small clods of dirt turn the water into lightly-muddied coffee.

The water's path is up and over, is down and around, is through. The water, too, may not remember.

**Wrong Turn**

I get lost every day now.
Dried fruit falls from the vine and stains.
Yes, something visible remains.

I grasp whatever drops on the floor nearby.
Plastic bottles sparkle miniature boats.
I cling to what floats by.

I have a few memories that slide
from the organ file—hard-crusted jewels;
remind me where I got them?

Have you seen a brain—its odd nooks and crannies,
its frightened softness like a newborn chick hiding
under a potato chip bag?

I have a few memories that elide for convenience's
sake. Strawberries and peaches collide—what a mess.
Have you seen my brain cluck, cluck, clucking?

Two or three wrong turns, and the journey folds in
on itself like my brain. On the way home, I try to forget
how little remains.

**Suture**

One theory goes—that which stops bleeding
signals healing. So stamp on the suture
till it oozes. This is no time for forgetting.

Stamp till you remember what blood
tastes like—rotting leaves, green mold, and
canned beets. Taste till you can't escape it.

*It's too much* you think. *That's enough* you
yell. Not possible. You thought you'd healed before,
yet you've forgotten over and over.

Stamp now. Stamp until your foot
is outlined on your body.

## Drawn Blood

I was having blood drawn again—a whole vial—*
no a whole liter, then a whole bathtub.

I was in a patient's gown.
I was in a bathrobe.
I was in a body bag.

I was in a bloodmobile,
strapped. I was in a bathtub
baking in movie lights.
I was wrapped in plastic to make real
what wasn't.

I was giving blood like an anti-Jesus—
to save myself.

Not even the heat, which had started to cook
the plastic, was a tourniquet for the blood
spill. My self-image reddened around the edges.
Before long, I noticed a whole country had poured
out of me—states I hadn't visited, borders
for unexplored places that scared me shitless.

*Part of the first line was borrowed from "Vial" by Mikko Harvey

**Tug of War**

The traffic is always circling—
welcome as the latest family of noisome Canada geese.

My therapist asks me if this is the start of an anxiety
poem. No, the traffic can be soothing in a rhythmic way—

*as long as one remains behind the thick, thick glass,* I added
in my head.

But I meant it. I found I could sit still for handfuls of minutes
as the cars pulled by like a losing team in a (Beckettian)

tug-of-war. And then the cars would clear out,
followed sporadically by others that tried but never made

the team—still not even realizing the war had ended.
*(The war has ended, hasn't it?)*

But what the hell! I know another is not far behind but worry
I won't see it coming. *Why do I need to see it coming?*

And despite the soothing flow of heavy traffic, anxiety
caulks the arteries in my neck.

**Missing #2**

I take a lock of my hair to use as a bookmark.
Day after day, as the pages are turned, the marker
separates and thins. Every day I turn
the pages and break off in little pieces.
I separate and thin.

I'm obsessed with what leaves my body,
what leaves and what's taken. The liquids
dry; the solids flake and drift. I'm obsessed
with how I separate, how I thin.

This story isn't difficult but isn't easy.
My text is middle-aged and collapsing.
My pages develop a second storyline—
the front becomes the back, the back
the front, and the story bleeds into itself—
now half the size it was.

I write this story until the words are too thin to read.
I write but leave only stray marks.
My narrative becomes a recovery mission.
I write to gain weight.

## Perspectives on Goldfish

My therapist suggests I forgive
the people who have distorted me.
I say I need fun house mirrors.

I begin to practice self-acceptance,
conjuring maximum distortions.
I need to own my freak. I practice
a lolling tongue, eyes rolling
in different directions.

It's the way I see what's hidden.
*I might just be crazy enough to tell
people who you really are.*
Then I get bored with myself.

I once photographed plastic apples
through the bottom of a bowl. The apples
looked like gold fish swimming.
I wanted to swim too. I moved closer
and closer until my perspective dissolved,
my camera lens no longer focused.

My therapist was impressed when
I showed up the next week as a goldfish.
He offered me congratulations and a glass of water.

## Some Things Have Seen Better Days

I found a twisted penny in a rain puddle.
It looked like a tortured body, edges
jagged as torn sandpaper. It's motto
mutilated too: In od We Rust.

I thought of the hands it passed through
city to countryside, cash register to nightstand.
It clinked as it joined the coins in my pocket like

animal bones tossed on motley-shaped patches
of hide exposed to November's bite.
Should I save one for my living room wall?

Later, kicking off clumps of dirt as you returned
from a day's gardening, you told me you'd found
a spade caked in dried blood in the shed
the weekend you moved into your house.

Your husband suggested keeping it
as evidence. *Of what,* you asked?
*Of something gone terribly wrong.*
You held that in your head
like a vessel about to rupture.

Kevin Hinkle is a poet, visual artist, and educator based primarily in New Jersey, USA. His poetry and visual art have been published in numerous literary and arts journals including *Impossible Archetype* (Ireland), *SurVision* (Ireland), *Naugatuck River Review, The Tishman Review, Baltimore Review, Tupelo Quarterly, Tulane Review, Grey Sparrow, Pedestal Magazine,* and *Utter,* several of these in conjunction with the poet, Michael McKeown Bondhus. Hinkle and Bondhus also conceived and curated an ekphrastic exhibition, *Garden State Hybrids* (combining Hinkle's visual art and poetry from NJ writers), which was exhibited in Somerville, NJ by the Somerset County Historical Commission.

Besides literary publications, Hinkle's work has been exhibited in many juried art shows including ones at Marin MOCA (CA), the Center for Contemporary Art (Bedminster, NJ), Montclair Art Museum's Affordable Art Fair (NJ), the Center for Visual Arts (Summit, NJ) the Perkins Center for the Arts (Moorestown, NJ), as well as in exhibits in New York (where he received an Honorable Mention in Soho Photo's Small Works exhibit), Maryland, Virginia, and North Carolina.

Hinkle's work can be found in numerous private collections as well as in the corporate art collection of PNC Bank.

www.ingramcontent.com/pod-product-compliance
Lightning Source LLC
LaVergne TN
LVHW041521070426
835507LV00012B/1726